Misconceptions about AIDS

Mohammad Nazmul Hasan Maziz

ISBN: 9798517540065

CONTENTS

1 Chapter One 1

2 Chapter Two 5

3 Chapter Three 8

4 Chapter Four 12

5 Chapter Five 22

6 Conclusion 28

7 References 29

8 Appendices 35

CHAPTER ONE

Introduction

1.1 Background

Today HIV is one of the largest epidemics in the world. The main aim of this study was to compare the knowledge and misconceptions of the Health Science students and Non-Health Science students regarding HIV/AIDS in a Private University in Selangor, Malaysia.

HIV/AIDS is not something one should take lightly [3]. With only 5 percent of the Eastern and Southern African, it is home to half of the world's population living with HIV [3]. In recent decades, HIV/AIDS has been working its magic up into society, spreading like an unstoppable cancer, almost to the point of it being immortal [3]. Due to this fact alone, students of the community must have the right and ample knowledge regarding this matter, aside from having a positive attitude towards both the illness and the victims of this very disease [3]. Misconceptions of HIV/AIDS when encountered throughout one's life line (career) can lead to serious mishaps [3]. In other words, they would not know how to deal with the problem professionally [3].

Due to lack of adequate information, youths are more exposed to infection as they engage in risky sexual practices [27]. It is of utter importance that both Health Science and Non- Health Science undergrads are equipped with the knowledge of HIV/AIDS. This is because having the knowledge of HIV/AIDS would benefit oneself to brace for what is coming if plagued by the dreaded malady [3].

Having good general public perception towards the possible causes of HIV infection serves as a tool to create better health care programs encouraging empathy towards victims [3]. However, these studies have been limited to compare integrated knowledge and misconceptions of the Health Science and Non-Health Science students. Few studies have examined potential differences in knowledge, risk perception and misconception towards HIV/AIDS. This study was conducted among the Health Science and Non-Health Science students because University students are amongst population in the age groups with the highest probability of acquiring HIV/AIDS as they are not aware of HIV risks [13].

The first HIV case in Malaysia was detected in 1986 [11]. Since then, the cumulative number of HIV infections up to June 2007 shows an amount of 78,784 cases [11]. The rapid increase of HIV/AIDS among young people is an alarming fact [11]. As a moderate Islamic country, Malaysia has majority of Muslim Malays and other ethnicities such as Chinese and Indian living together with religious freedom. Topics such as sex and sexually transmitted infections (STIs) are considered taboo and sensitive, and usually are not discussed openly. Although Malaysians are mostly conservative and strictly hold on to their traditional values, the younger generation engage in unprotected sexual intercourse [11]. The cumulative number of HIV cases in Malaysia went up to 101,672 cases by the end of 2013 [29].

1.2 Problem statement and study justification

In Malaysia, talks and awareness programs about HIV/AIDS are held at secondary schools regularly. However, there are new cases of HIV/AIDS arising among people every year. This could be caused by low level of knowledge regarding HIV/AIDS. This shows that the awareness programs held at school levels alone is not enough to prevent this disease from spreading. Thus, the knowledge and misconceptions about this disease among university students should also be assessed. Health Science students have a better exposure to gaining knowledge about this disease since it is a part of their curriculum whereas it is not the case for Non-Health Science students. Thus, this study is carried out to compare knowledge and misconceptions among the Health Science students and Non-Health Science students about HIV/AIDS in a Private University in Selangor, Malaysia.

1.3 Objective
General Objectives
To study the Comparison of Knowledge and Misconceptions among Health Science students and Non-Health Science students concerning about HIV and AIDS in a Private University in Selangor, Malaysia.

Specific Objectives:
- To study the general knowledge and misconceptions about HIV/AIDS.
- To compare the knowledge between Health-Science students and Non-Health Science students.
- To compare the misconceptions between Health-Science students and Non-Health Science students.

Alternative Hypothesis
- The knowledge among the Health Science students is higher than the Non-Health Science students.
- The misconception among the Health Science students is lower than the Non-Health Science students.

Null Hypothesis
- There is no difference in knowledge among the Health Science students and Non-Health Science students.
- There is no difference in misconceptions among the Health Science student and Non-Health Science students

CHAPTER TWO

Literature Review

Based on the cross sectional study done on 340 preclinical and clinical students in a public university in Malaysia, it was shown that clinical students felt more discomfort in handling HIV/AIDS patients compared to preclinical students [4]. Another study was conducted using questionnaires among 327 medical students from third, fourth and fifth year, in universities around Klang Valley. It showed that majority of the participants were aware of the mode of transmissions such as perinatal transmission, and homosexuality. A few students showed negative attitude such as uncertainty in being close to HIV patients [9]. Another study was done in the year 2014 to determine the level of knowledge of pre-medical students and the change in their attitude throughout their preclinical years in Israel. A questionnaire was used to test the knowledge of transmission of HIV, basic knowledge of its treatment and the attitude of the 1470 participants. Generally, preclinical medical students are highly knowledgeable. Most misconceptions were on transmission of the virus through breastfeeding and post exposure prophylaxis. The attitude of the students toward the disease was mostly associated with negative feelings such as shame and fear and no positive change was noticed. Measures should be implemented to improve the attitude of the students [3].

A recent cross sectional study was conducted to investigate the level of awareness and the willingness of physiotherapy students to treat HIV/AIDS patient, in Banarsidas Chandiwala Institute of Physiotherapy, New Delhi, India using 217 participants who were all physiotherapy students. Despite having a good knowledge on the disease, negative attitude was shown by the students toward HIV/AIDS patients. This negative attitude was driven by the fear of getting infected by the virus.

The students should be enlightened on the importance of giving treatment to HIV patients [5]. In the United Arab Emirates, a cross sectional study was done to evaluate the awareness, attitude and educational requirement among the university students. The participants were made up of 119 males and 148 females. More than half of the participants believed that school did not provide sufficient information about the disease and more information can be gained from the media or books. Males were more knowledgeable while females showed higher compassion and agreed that premarital testing is a way to protect them from infection. Youngsters should be educated on prevention of HIV [6]. A facilitator-guided self-administered questionnaire was used to conduct a cross sectional study to assess comprehensive HIV/AIDS knowledge among students from 14 high schools in different districts of eastern Ethiopia. The results showed that only a quarter of the students have a wide knowledge on HIV/AIDS. Compared to male students, the female students have lesser knowledge about HIV/AIDS [7].

In year 2014, 556 students from two universities participated in a cross sectional study conducted to assess HIV/AIDS comprehensive & correct knowledge among Sudanese university students. 2.9% of the participants have not heard of the disease. The rate of knowledge was poor, especially among the female participants. About 50% of the students did not know the ways to prevent the disease [1].

Using 4981 Health Science and 8,061 Non-Health Science students, a cross-sectional survey was done in 17 universities in 17 low and middle income countries across Asia to study differences in health risk behavior and knowledge between Health Science and Non-Health Science university students. Results show that both category students had the same mean number of health risk behaviors. Health science students were more aware of health behavior risks (5.5) than Non-Health Science students (4.6). No association was found between risk awareness and health risk behavior among the two groups [30].

CHAPTER THREE

Materials and Methods

3.1 Study design

This is a descriptive, cross sectional study that was conducted via a self-administered questionnaire among Health Science and Non-Health Science students in a Private University located in Selangor, Malaysia.

3.2 Study population

The study population includes undergraduate students from. All the students were informed about the study design. Those who agreed to participate were authorized.

3.3 Sample Size

The study sample size was 180 among which 90 are Health Science students (30 Malay, 30 Chinese and 30 Indians) and 90 are Non-Health Science students (30 Malay, 30 Chinese and 30 Indians).

3.4 Inclusion and exclusion criteria

The inclusion criteria include all Malaysian students aged 18-25 years old, of the three major races (Malay, Chinese and Indian) of both genders male and female and who were willing to provide written consent. The students under 18 and those above 25 or those not willing to participate and are not able to provide written consent were excluded from this study.

3.5 Study survey instrument

A self-administered validated questionnaire [12] was used with the permission of the publishing author. The questionnaire collected the demographics of the participants and it also consists of five other different domains that gave us a clear idea. The questionnaire consists of 43 questions with a fixed response answering key. The questionnaire consists of 5 parts which are as follows, Part A is related to respondent's socio-demographic background (7 items), Part B relevant to knowledge regarding HIV/AIDS (5 statements), Part C on risk perception towards possible causes of HIV/AIDS (14 statements), Part D on respondent's views about measure to prevent HIV transmissions (12 statements) and Part E on misconceptions towards HIV/AIDS (5 statements).

3.6 Data Collection

The data collection was done from 3rd to 31st July 2017. The self-administered questionnaire [12] was distributed and collected from groups of students by the five investigators. The participants took approximately 5-10 minutes to fill up the questionnaire completely. The participants signed a consent form which included information about purpose, importance and procedure of the study.

3.7 Statistical analysis plan

All statistical analyses were performed using SPSS (version 23). Descriptive statistics were conducted to describe all the continuous (mean and standard deviation) and categorical variables (frequency distributions and percentages). The differences in the total mean score between the two groups (Health Science and Non-Health science) were compared using the Chi-square test. A two-tailed p-value of <0.05 was regarded as statistically significant.

3.8 Ethical consideration

The questionnaire was used with the consent of the author. Ethical clearance was obtained from that University. Brief explanation about the study was provided at the cover page of the questionnaires while instructions were stated clearly to the participants on how to fill it up. Written consent form was obtained from all the participants. They were informed that participation was voluntary. All information provided in questionnaire would be kept confidential and data will be used only for research purposes. Participants were reminded not to write their name and other personal identification numbers on the forms. All participants were free to withdraw from study at any time. Strict anonymity and confidentiality was maintained throughout the process of data collection and analysis.

3.9 List of dependent variables and independent variables

Dependent Variables:

- Knowledge
- Misconceptions

Independent Variables:

- Age
- Gender
- Marital status
- Religious beliefs
- Nationality
- Race
- Study course
- Academic year

CHAPTER FOUR

Results

The demographic characteristics of the total participants are presented in Table 4.1. The evaluation was conducted with 180 students of both Health Science and Non-Health Science.

Table 4.1: Demographic characteristics of the total participants (n=180)

Characteristics	Total (n=180)	Health Science (n=90)	Non-Health Science (n=90)
Age (y), mean (±SD)	21.23 (±1.695)	21.18 (±1.481)	21.08 (±1.892)
Gender, n (%)			
Male	53 (29.4%)	26 (28.9%)	27 (30.0%)
Female	127 (70.6%)	64 (71.1%)	63 (70.0%)
Marital status			
Single	180(100%)	90 (100%)	90 (100%)
Married	0 (0%)	0 (0%)	0 (0%)
Widowed	0 (0%)	0 (0%)	0 (0%)
Divorced	0 (0%)	0 (0%)	0 (0%)
Separated	0 (0%)	0 (0%)	0 (0%)
Religion			
Muslim	65 (36.1%)	35 (38.9)	30 (33.3%)
Christian	28 (15.6%)	15 (16.7)	13 (14.4%)
Buddhist	43 (23.9%)	17 (18.9)	26 (28.9%)
Hindu	40 (22.2%)	21 (23.3)	19 (21.1%)
Others	4 (2.2%)	2 (2.2)	2 (2.2%)
Race			
Malay	60 (33.3%)	30 (33.3%)	30 (33.3%)
Chinese	60 (33.3%)	30 (33.3%)	30 (33.3%)
Indian	60 (33.3%)	30 (33.3%)	30 (33.3%)

SD denotes standard deviation, n denotes number of participants, y denotes years

The mean age of the total participants was 21.23 years and its standard deviation is 1.695 years. Among the participants, 90 of them were Health Science students (50%) and 90 of them were Non- Health Science students (50%). The participants were composed of 53 (29.4%) males and 127 (70.6%) females. The participants were all Malaysians from the three major races in Malaysia (Malay n=60, Chinese n=60 and Indian n=60). The marital status of all participants is single. Among all the 180 participant's majority of them were Muslims 65 (36.1%) followed by Buddhists 43 (23.9%), Hindus 40 (22.2%), Christians 28 (15.6%) and others (2.2%).

Table 4.2 below represents all the correct answers to the questionnaire as given by the author of the questionnaire. The reference for the following tables was taken from the above table to determine the percentages of answers answered correctly and wrongly by the respondents.

Table 4.2: Correct answers for the questionnaires

Variables	Correct Answer
General knowledge	
1. AIDS abbreviation	Yes
2. AIDS a transmittable disease	Yes
3. AIDS a hereditary disease	No
4. AIDS cured at this moment	No
5. There is a vaccine for AIDS Attitudes	No
General public perception	
6. Sexual intercourse without a condom with HIV-infected person	Yes
7. Sharing needle with HIV-infected organ	Yes
8 Transfusion of HIV-infected blood or receiving HIV-infected organ	Yes
9. Having sex with multiple sexual partners with unknown HIV status	Yes
10. From an HIV positive mother to her foetus	Yes
11. Sharing personal items such as shaving blades	Yes
12. Breast Feeding from a HIV-infected mother	Yes
13. Having tattoo or body piercing	No
14. Kissing can transmit HIV-infection	No
15. Mosquito bites	No
16. Sharing/eating a meal with a HIV-infected person	No
17. Sharing water or drinks with an HIV-infected person	No
18. Using Public toilets	No
19. Casual contacts with an HIV-infected person	No

Respondents views

20. Avoid taking illicit drugs/ use of intravenous drugs	Yes
21. By avoiding sharing needles and syringes	Yes
22. Having sex with only one faithful, uninfected partner	Yes
23. Using condoms during sexual intercourse	Yes
24. Treating STDs promptly	Yes
25. Screening donated blood before transfusion	Yes
26. Not sharing toilets with an infected person	No
27. Not sharing food with an infected person	No
28. Isolating people living with HIV/AIDS	No
29. Do not stay with infected person on same house	No
30. Do not have casual contact with infected person	No
31. Avoid mosquito bites for HIV transmission	No
Misconceptions	
32. Love is a reason for HIV/AIDS	No
33. AIDS is a punishment of God	No
34. AIDS can treat by holy water	No
53. AIDS do not come after marriage	No
36. AIDS can be transmitted by the cough	No

The frequency and percentage of correct answers and wrong answers among the participants based on faculty of the students were reported in Table 4.3.

Table 4.3: Questions on general knowledge on HIV/AIDS

Variables	Correct Answers		Wrong Answers		p-value
	Health Science	Non-Health Science	Health Science	Non-Health Science	
General Knowledge					
1. AIDS abbreviation	84 (46.7%)	57 (31.7%)	6 (3.3%)	33 (18.3%)	0.000
2. AIDS a transmittable disease	85 (47.2%)	75 (41.7%)	5 (2.8%)	15 (8.3%)	0.018
3. AIDS a hereditary disease	63 (35.0%)	36 (20.0%)	27 (15.0%)	54 (30.0%)	0.000
4. AIDS cured at this moment	82 (45.6%)	74 (41.1%)	8 (4.4%)	16 (8.9%)	0.079
5. There is a vaccine for AIDS Attitudes	64 (35.6%)	47 (26.1%)	26 (14.4%)	43 (23.9%)	0.009

The table showed that among the 5 questions regarding the general knowledge for HIV/AIDS, all the frequency and also the percentage of correct answers was higher in Health Science students (30.0%-50.0%) as compared to Non-Health Science students (20.0%-45.0%). In other words, the frequency and percentage of wrong answers was higher in Non-Health Science students (5.0%-30.0%) than in Health Science students (4.4%-15.0%). For example, the third variable, "Is AIDS a hereditary disease?", the frequency and percentage of correct answers for Health-Science students and Non-Health Science students were 65 (35.0%) and 36 (20.0%) respectively, while for the wrong answers were 27 (15.0%) and 54 (30.0%) respectively. Moreover, the p-value is 0. It showed that there is a significant difference between the answers given by Health-Science students and also Non-Health Science students. For all the 5 questions of general knowledge about HIV/AIDS, there were significant difference shown in each question except for the fourth questions because its p-value is 0.079 which is greater than 0.05, while for others are 0, 0.018, 0 and 0.009.

Table 4.4 also shows the frequency and percentage of correct answers and wrong answers among the participants based on faculty of the students (Health Science and Non-Health Science). There are 14 questions related to the general public perception towards HIV/AIDS.

Table 4.4: Questions related to the General Public Perception

Variables	Correct answers		Wrong answers		p-value
	Health Science	Non-Health Science	Health Science	Non-Health Science	
General public perception					
1. Sexual intercourse without a condom with HIV-infected person	87 (48.3%)	80 (44.4%)	3 (1.7%)	10 (5.6%)	0.044
2. Sharing needle with HIV-infected people	90 (100.0%)	82 (45.6%)	0 (0.0%)	8 (4.4%)	0.004
3 Transfusion of HIV-infected blood or receiving HIV-infected organ	89 (49.4%)	80 (44.4%)	1 (0.6%)	10 (5.6%)	0.005
4. Having sex with multiple sexual partners with unknown HIV status	89 (49.4%)	77 (42.8%)	1 (0.6%)	13 (7.2%)	0.001
5. From an HIV positive mother to her foetus	87 (48.3%)	65 (36.1%)	3 (1.7%)	25 (13.9%)	0.000
6. Sharing personal items such as shaving blades	73 (40.6%)	55 (30.6%)	17 (9.4%)	35 (19.4%)	0.003
7. Breast Feeding from a HIV-infected mother	65 (36.1%)	67 (37.2%)	25 (13.9%)	23 (12.8%)	0.736
8. Having tattoo or body piercing	26 (14.4%)	57 (31.7%)	64 (35.6%)	33 (18.3%)	0.000
9. Kissing can transmit HIV-infection	67 (37.2%)	58 (32.2%)	23 (12.8%)	32 (17.8%)	0.145
10. Mosquito bites	61 (33.9%)	52 (28.9%)	29 (16.1%)	38 (21.1%)	0.165
11. Sharing/eating a meal with a HIV-infected person	80 (44.4%)	59 (32.8%)	10 (5.6%)	31 (17.2%)	0.000
12. Sharing water or drinks with an HIV-infected person	76 (42.2%)	61 (33.9%)	14 (7.8%)	29 (16.1%)	0.009
13. Using Public toilets	76 (42.2%)	81 (45.0%)	14 (7.8%)	9 (5.0%)	0.264
14. Casual contacts (hugging or touching) with an HIV-infected person	85 (47.2%)	82 (45.6%)	5 (2.8%)	8 (4.4%)	0.388

Majority of the data showed that Health Science students had a higher percentage (30.0%-100.0%) of correct answers when compared to Non-Health Science students (50.0%-90.0%).

Out of 14 questions, there were 9 questions (1, 2, 3, 4 ,5 ,6 ,8 ,11, 12) showing significant differences among the answers given by Health Science students and Non-Health Science students because the *p*-value for the 9 questions were 0.044, 0.004, 0.005, 0.001, 0, 0.003, 0, 0 and 0.009 respectively which is lower than 0.05. However, the remaining 5 questions (7, 9, 10, 13, 14) did not show significant difference because their *p*-value were more than 0.05 (0.736, 0.145, 0.165, 0.264, 0.388 respectively).

In Table 4.5 below, the frequency and percentage of correct and wrong answers among the participants based on faculty of students were reported (Health Science and Non Health Science Students). The table showed the 12 questions asking about the respondent's views about HIV/AIDS.

Table 4.5: Questions about respondent's views about HIV/AIDS

Variables	Correct answers		Wrong answers		*p*-value
	Health Science	Non-Health Science	Health Science	Non-Health Science	
Respondents views					
1. Avoid taking illicit drugs/ use of intravenous drugs	84 (46.7%)	78 (43.3%)	6 (3.3%)	12 (6.7%)	0.136
2. By avoiding sharing needles and syringes	89 (49.4%)	84 (46.7%)	1 (0.6%)	6 (3.3%)	0.054
3. Having sex with only one faithful, uninfected partner	89 (49.4%)	79 (43.9%)	1 (0.6%)	11 (6.1%)	0.003
4. Using condoms during sexual intercourse	88 (48.9%)	77 (42.8%)	2 (1.1%)	13 (7.2%)	0.003
5. Treating STDs promptly	87 (48.3%)	76 (42.2%)	3 (1.7%)	14 (7.8%)	0.005
6. Screening donated blood before transfusion	87 (48.3%)	83 (46.1%)	3 (1.7%)	7 (3.9%)	0.193
7. Not sharing toilets with an infected person	73 (40.6%)	60 (33.3%)	17 (9.4%)	30 (16.7%)	0.027
8. Not sharing food with an infected person	74 (41.1%)	56 (31.1%)	16 (8.9%)	34 (18.9%)	0.003
9. Isolating people living with HIV/AIDS	75 (41.7%)	52 (28.9%)	15 (8.3%)	38 (21.1%)	0.000
10. Do not stay with infected person on same house	81 (45.0%)	61 (33.9%)	9 (5.0%)	29 (16.1%)	0.000
11. Do not have casual contact with infected person	80 (44.4%)	67 (37.2%)	10 (5.6%)	23 (12.8%)	0.012
12. Avoid mosquito bites for HIV transmission	62 (34.4%)	52 (28.9%)	28 (15.6%)	38 (21.1%)	0.122

All the frequency and percentage of correct answers was higher in Health Science Students compared to Non-Health Science Students and vice versa for the wrong answers. Generally, the views of the both the groups (Health Science and Non-Health Science) were regarded as almost similar in comparison. For all the 12 questions of respondents views about HIV/AIDS, there was significant difference shown in each question except for the questions 1,6 and 12 because its respective *p*-value which are 0.136, 0.193 and 0.122 are greater than 0.05.

In Table 4.6, the frequency and percentage of correct and wrong answers among the participants based on their faculties are reported (Health Science and Non Health Science Students). The table showed 5 questions related to the misconceptions about HIV/AIDS.

Table 4.6: Questions on misconceptions about HIV/AIDS

Variables	Correct answers		Wrong answers		*p*-value
	Health Science	Non-Health Science	Health Science	Non-Health Science	
Misconceptions					
1. Love is a reason for HIV/AIDS	81 (45.0%)	76 (42.2%)	9 (5.0%)	14 (7.8%)	0.264
2. AIDS is a punishment of God	80 (44.4%)	65 (36.1%)	10 (5.6%)	25 (13.9%)	0.005
3. AIDS can treat by holy water	85 (47.2%)	82 (45.6%)	5 (2.8%)	8 (4.4%)	0.388
4. AIDS do not come after marriage	79 (43.9%)	71 (39.4%)	11 (6.1%)	19 (10.6%)	0.110
5. AIDS can be transmitted by the cough	81 (45.0%)	70 (38.9%)	9 (5.0%)	20 (11.1%)	0.026

All the frequency and percentage of correct answers was higher in Health Science Students compared to Non-Health Science Students and vice versa for the wrong answers. The majority of Health Science respondents had less misconception about HIV/AIDS, with 75-85% correctly answering the five statements. However, many misconceptions were still noted relating to HIV/AIDS, such as "AIDS is a punishment of God", "AIDS can be transmitted by cough" and "AIDS do not come after marriage" which at least of more than 10% of Non-Health Sciences Students had answered incorrectly. Furthermore, for the 5 questions on misconceptions about HIV/AIDS, there were significant differences shown in the questions 2 and 5 where the *p*-values were 0.005 and 0.26 respectively except for the questions 1, 3 and 4 as the *p*-values were 0.264, 0.388 and 0.110 respectively.

The Table 4.7 represented the mean and standard deviation of all the other tables (Table 4.3, 4.4, 4.5 and 4.6). Graph 1 showed the overall view of percentage of correct answers and wrong answers given by Health Science students and Non-Health Science students.

Table 4.7: Total Average of All Variables

Variables	Correct answers		Wrong answers	
	Health Science	Non-Health Science	Health Science	Non-Health Science
General Knowledge	42.02% (±0.062)	32.12% (±0.094)	7.98% (±0.062)	17.88% (±0.094)
General Public Perception	45.27% (±0.182)	37.94% (±0.064)	8.31% (0.095)	12.06% (±0.064)
Respondent Views	44.85% (±0.046)	38.19% (±0.067)	5.15% (±0.046)	11.81% (±0.067)
Misconceptions	45.10% (±0.013)	40.44% (±0.036)	4.90% (±0.013)	9.56% (±0.036)
Mean (±SD)	44.31% (±0.015)	37.17% (±0.036)	6.59% (±0.018)	12.83% (±0.036)

SD denotes standard deviation

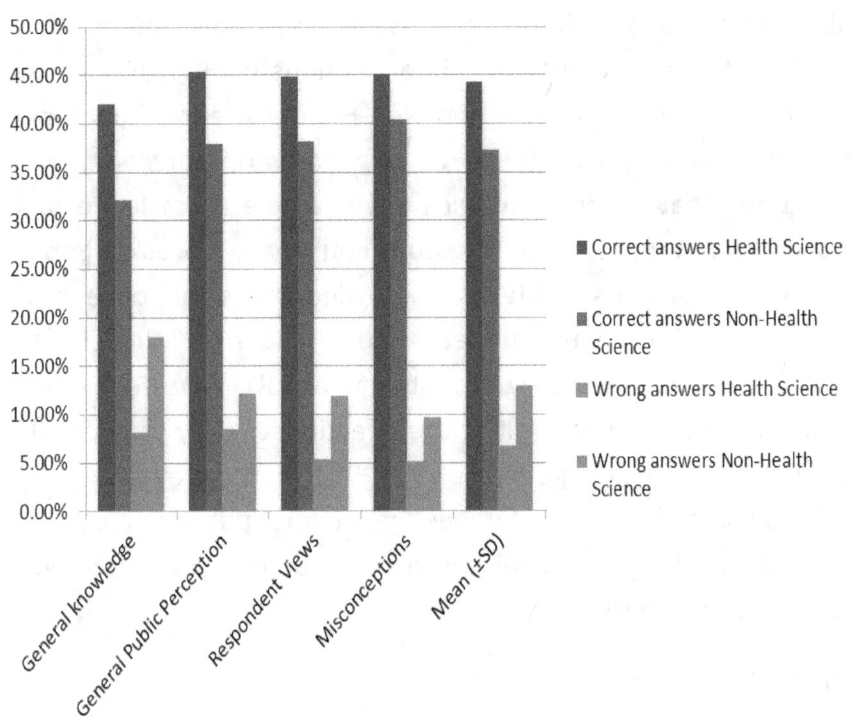

It shows that the Health Science students generally had a higher percentage of correct answer with a mean and standard deviation of 44.31% and 0.015 respectively, whereas the Non-Health Science students had a higher percentage of wrong answers with a mean and standard deviation of 12.83% and 0.036 respectively.

CHAPTER FIVE

Discussion

This is the first descriptive, cross-sectional study conducted to compare the knowledge and misconceptions of HIV/AIDS among the Health-Science students and Non-Health Science students in that University. Since HIV is a very common infection, it is important that people should have ample knowledge and awareness about HIV/AIDS. This study could have a positive impact on raising awareness of HIV/AIDS knowledge and misconceptions among undergraduate students in Malaysian Universities. Educational awareness programs about HIV/AIDS have been one of the key measures in controlling the infection, as they promote the healthy life style of the general public [10]. The study reveals several findings about the general knowledge, general public perceptions, respondent's views and misconceptions among Health Science students and also Non-Health Students.

General knowledge

The respondents of both branches (Health Science students and Non-Health Science students) have a clear understanding about the abbreviation used for HIV/AIDS which was about 78% of the participants. The Health Science students (35%-47%) have more correct answer and thus have a better knowledge of HIV/AIDS than the Non-Health Science students (26%-41%). Based on the results on Table 4.2, it shows a high percentage of correct answers of Health Science students (47.2%) and Non-Health Science students (41.7%) have knowledge on issues related to HIV/AIDS transmission. Both the groups had good knowledge about AIDS which cannot be cured having a high percentage (41%-46%) of correct answer.

Also, the notation that "AIDS is a hereditary disease" and "there is a vaccine for AIDS", the Health Science percentage of answering correctly was higher as compared to Non-Health Science percentage. In our study, however about 20%-35% of the respondents thought that AIDS is not a hereditary disease whereas about 26%-36% of the respondents thought there was no vaccine available for AIDS. Thus, overall the respondents had good knowledge about the abbreviation of AIDS, AIDS transmission and its curing except they lack knowledge of AIDS being a hereditary disease and whether there is a vaccine available for AIDS. A similar study was conducted in Tanzania; it spoke about three quarters of the respondents demonstrating comprehensive knowledge about HIV/AIDS [24]. In contrast, a study conducted in Saudi Arabia showed the overall mean knowledge score of the respondents was 5.2 correct answers out of 9. However, in this study a low knowledge level of HIV/AIDS was found among the medical and non-medical students [22]. Another study that was conducted among Sudanese University students stated that the participants had poor knowledge about HIV/AIDS [23]. Therefore, it is important to consider taking initiative in setting up various centres in order to instil a basic knowledge about the disease all around the world so that as to eliminate the stigma surrounding this disease.

General public perceptions about HIV/AIDS

For the questions regarding the general public's perception, many Health Science students in that University had a wrong perception about having a tattoo or body piercing could transmit HIV/AIDS which is the same finding as the research done in urban African Americans in the South [16].

From previous researches [2,14], their research found out that most of the people were having misconceptions that "kissing could transmit HIV" which is the same with our research finding, 23 (12.8%) students from Health Science and 32 (17.8%) students from Non-Health Science for the frequency and percentage for their wrong answer which was actually very high. Moreover, quite a number of Health Science students also had misconceptions about "breastfeeding from a HIV-infected mother could transmit the disease" and that "Mosquito bites could transmit HIV". These misconceptions were the same as the research which had been done in a Nigerian Teaching Hospital [17]. 59.5% of the study population in the research of Maimaiti N et al answered that HIV could be transmitted through mosquito bites [24]. On the other hand, Non-Health Science students mostly had an incorrect perception about "Mosquito bites", "Sharing personal items such as shaving blades" and "Having tattoo and body piercing could transmit HIV." Through data analysis, there were three quarter of the questions showing significant difference between the answers given by Health Science students and Non-Health Science students. Students' perception about HIV/AIDS should be corrected because it is very important for them to prevent infection from HIV.

Respondent views about preventive measures

For this section, Health Science students had higher frequencies and also percentages of correct answers for all the 12 questions as compared to Non-Health Science students. The questions which Health Science students had very low frequency and percentages of correct answers were on the questions such as "Avoid mosquito bites for HIV transmission" (62 & 34.4%) and "Not sharing toilets with an infected person" (73 & 40.6%). In the previous research, there were 21.2% answers the question "Avoiding mosquito bites" correctly with is lower percentage than us [2]. Moreover, another study carried in a public university in Malaysia showed that more than half of their participants (77.4%) trusted that HIV infection could be transmitted through public toilet. This also proved that there were misconceptions among the students in public university of Malaysia [28]. In contrast, most of the Non-Health Science students got incorrect answers in questions like isolating people living with HIV/AIDS (52 & 28,.9%) and avoid mosquito bites for HIV transmission (52 & 28.9%). There were also same misconceptions happened as the research carried in Mahatma Gandhi Memorial [2] and also researched carried out by Unal Ayranci in a Turkish population [26]. Overall, more than half of the Health Science students and Non-Health Science students answered the 12 questions correctly. This shows that most of the students in that University have a correct mind set on preventive measures for HIV/AIDS.

Misconceptions

Misconception about HIV may cause a negative attitude towards people suffering from this serious disease that could lead to serious harm on their physical and emotional state. Misconception is a major barrier to control and prevent the spread of AIDS [19,20].

In a conservative country like Malaysia where it is not encouraged to talk about sexual issues, the expected rate of misconceptions was very high. This is also the same with other conservative countries like Sudan for example where it is rare for parents to discuss sensitive topics such as STDs with family members [18]. But our study revealed that most of the respondents didn't have a lot of misconceptions about HIV/AIDS. However, our findings showed that the Non-Health Science respondents had a higher percentage (9.56%) of misconceptions than the Health Science respondents (4.90%).

The statements that had the highest misconceptions from both populations were "AIDS is a punishment of God", "AIDS do not come after marriage" and "AIDS can be transmitted by the cough". Even though Malaysia is a religious country, for the statement "AIDS is a punishment of God" only few participants 10 (5.6%) from Health Science and 25 (13.9%) from Non-Health Science had incorrect answers. Other studies however, have shown that there was a higher percentage of people who believe that AIDS is a divine punishment from God [2,10]. Also comparing to a study done in Sudan for the statement "AIDS do not come after marriage", 11 (6.1%) participants of Health Science and 19(10.6%) participants of Non-Health Science answered incorrectly. Finally, for the statement "AIDS can be transmitted by the cough", 9 (5.0%) participants of health science and 20 (11.1%) of non-health science answered incorrectly. A study conducted earlier in Japan showed that fear, lack of knowledge, or religious beliefs, negative attitudes towards HIV/AIDS patients can lead to stigmatization of the disease [15]. It is very important to take action in order to get rid of these misconceptions that people have towards HIV and AIDS. South Africa has set an interesting example in implementing HIV/AIDS prevention programs including community-based HIV awareness programs and education campaigns, research on HIV prevention together with the introduction of anti-retroviral therapy (ART). This comprehensive approach has led to increased knowledge within the community which reduced the social stigma and led again to better uptake of voluntary counselling and HIV testing [21]. The Malaysian government could take up few of these above examples so as to create better awareness and knowledge among the population of the country.

Strength of the Study

The strength of the study is that the questions in the questionnaire can be addressed in a relatively short period of time. Secondly, an ethical and institutional approval was easily obtained as the study population was small. And since a small study population was used it saved a lot of cost of expenditure, time and resources than when using a larger study population.

Limitations of the study:

The limitations of the study were that using the stratified random sampling technique from a single university may not be able to represent the whole study population. One of the reasons for this was due to lack of time and resources; we were unable to have a large study population size. Another limitation was that some the participants showed lack of interest and did not take the questionnaire survey seriously thus it was not easy to assess if the students had any difficulty in understanding all the questions in the questionnaire.

Conclusion

This study draws a general picture of a Private University student population's knowledge and misconceptions towards HIV/AIDS. Though the university student population had a good knowledge background, there were few misconceptions that need to be addressed. Thus, this study was conducted to compare the knowledge and misconceptions among the two major branches (Health Science students and Non-Health Science students). However, the major findings of this study were that the Health Science students had better knowledge and fewer misconceptions when compared to Non-Health Science students. Furthermore, from the study we come to a conclusion that despite the knowledge that the students possess it is important to raise awareness about this disease, and this can be done by taking initiative in conducting campaigns, awareness programs, educational speeches, hosting fundraising events, produce information pamphlets and through social media awareness. It is equally important that both the study groups have adequate knowledge on this issue but since the Non-Health Science students had a higher level of misconception and a low level of knowledge when compared to the Health Science it is important to focus more on the Non-Health Science group.

References

1. Abdulateef Elbadawi and Hyder Mirghani. Assessment of HIV/AIDS comprehensive correct knowledge among Sudanese university: a cross-sectional analytic study 2014.   Pan Afr Med J. 2016; 24: 48. Published online 2016 May 11. doi: 10.11604/pamj.2016.24.48.8684

2. Akshaya Srikanth Bhagavathula, et al, A cross sectional study: the knowledge, attitude, perception, misconception and views (KAPMV) of adult family members of people living with human immune virus-HIV acquired immune deficiency syndrome-AIDS (PLWHA). Springerplus. 2015;4:769.

3. Baytner-Zamir R, Lorber M, Hermoni D. Assessment of the knowledge and attitudes regarding HIV/AIDS among pre-clinical medical students in Israel. BMC Res Notes. 2014 Mar 20 doi: 10.1186/1756-0500-7-168.

4. Chew BH, Cheong AT. Assessing HIV/AIDS Knowledge and Stigmatizing Attitudes among Medical Students in Universiti Putra Malaysia. Med J Malaysia. 2013;68(1):24-9.

5. Chugh P et al. Int J Community Med Public Health. 2017 Apr;4(4):1148-1153 International Journal of Community Medicine and Public Health | April 2017 | Vol 4 | Issue 4 Page 1148.

6. Maria Gańczak, Peter Barss, Fatima Alfaresi, Shamma Almazrouei, Amal Muraddad, Fatma Al-Maskari.Break the silence: HIV/AIDS knowledge, attitudes, and educational needs among Arab university students in United Arab Emirates. J

Adolesc. Health. 2007 Jun; 40(6): 572.e1–572.e8. Published online 2007 Mar 26. doi: 10.1016/j.jadohealth.2007.01.011

7. Lemessa Oljira, Yemane Berhane, and Alemayehu Worku. Assessment of comprehensive HIV/AIDS knowledge level among in-school adolescents in eastern Ethiopia. J Int AIDS Soc. 2013 Mar 20;16:17349. doi: 10.7448/IAS.16.1.17349.

8. Syed Imran Ahmed, Mohamed Azmi Hassali, Noorizan Abdul Aziz, Am J Pharm Educ. An Assessment of the Knowledge, Attitudes, and Risk Perceptions of Pharmacy Students Regarding HIV/AIDS.2009 Feb 19; 73(1): 15.

9. Verma RK, Wong S, Chakravarthi S, Barua A. An Assessment of the Level of Awareness. Attitudes and Opinions of the Medical Students Concerning HIV and AIDS in Malaysia. J Clin Diagn Res. 2014 Apr;8(4):HC10-3. doi: 10.7860/JCDR/2014/7829.4286.

10. Essam M Janahi, Sakina Mustafa, Sajeda Alsari, Mariam AL-Mannai, Ghada N Farhat, Public knowledge, perceptions, and attitudes towards HIV/AIDS in Bahrain: A cross-sectional study. J Infect Dev Ctries 2016; 10(9):1003-1011doi:10.3855/jidc.7665

11. Li-Pin Wong, Caroline-Kwong Leng Chin, Wah-Yun Low, and Nasruddin Jaafar. HIV/AIDS-Related Knowledge Among Malaysian Young Adults: Findings From a Nationwide survery. J Int AIDS Soc. 2008; 10: 148.

12. Akshaya Srikanth Bhagavathula et al. A cross sectional study: the knowledge, attitude, perception, misconception and views (KAPMV) of adult family members of people living with human

immune virus-HIV acquired immune deficiency syndrome-AIDS (PLWHA) Bhagavathula et al. SpringerPlus (2015) 4:769 DOI 10.1186/s40064-015-1541-2

13. Thana Khawcharoenporn et al. Uptake of HIV testing and counseling, risk perception and linkage to HIV care among Thaiuniversity students. BMC Public Health. 2016 Jul 12;16:556. doi: 10.1186/s12889-016-3274-8.

14. Yazdi CA, Aschbacher K, Arbantaj A, Naser HM, Abdollahi E, Asadi M, et al. Knowledge, attitude and sources of information regarding HIV/AIDS in Iranian adolescents. AIDS Care. 2006;18(8):1004–1010. doi: 10.1080/09540120500526284.

15. Guoqin Wang, Koji Wada, Keika Hoshi, Nanae Sasaki, Satoshi Ezoe, Toshihiko Satoh. Association of Knowledge of HIV and Other Factors with Individuals' Attitudes toward HIV Infection: A National Cross-Sectional Survey among the Japanese Non-Medical Working Population. July 16, 2013. https://doi.org/10.1371/journal.pone.0068495

16. H Klien, CE Sterk and KW Elifson. Knowledge about HIV in a Community Sample of Urban African Americans in the South. J AIDS Clin Res. 2016 Oct; 7(10): 622.

17. OI Opeodu, TJ Ogunrinde. Mode of Transmission of HIV/AIDS: Perception of Dental Patients in a Nigerian Teaching Hospital. J West Afr Coll Surg. 2015 Jan-Mar; 5(1): 1–19.

18. Abdool Karim Q, Meyer-Weitz, Harrison A. Interventions with youth in high prevalence areas. In: Mayer KH, Pizer HF, editors.

HIV preventions: A comprehensive approach. London: Academic Press; 2009.

19. Corrigan PW, Penn DL. Lessons from social psychology on discrediting psychiatric stigma. Am Psychol. 1999 Sep;54(9):765–76. [PubMed]

20. Lieber E, Li L, Wu Z, Rotheram-Borus MJ, Guan J, National Institute of Mental Health Collaborative HIV Prevention Trial Group HIV/STD stigmatization fears as health-seeking barriers in China. AIDS Behav. 2006 Sep;10(5):463–71. [PMC free article] [PubMed]

21. Mall, S., Middelkoop, K., Mark, D., Wood, R., and Bekker, L.G. Changing patterns in HIV/AIDS stigma and uptake of voluntary counselling and testing services: the results of two consecutive community surveys conducted in the Western Cape, South Africa. AIDS Care. 2013; 25: 194–201

22. Heba Abdullah Alwafi et al. Knowledge and attitudes toward HIV/AIDS among the general population of Jeddah, Saudi Arabia. http://dx.doi.org/10.1016/j.jiph.2017.04.005.

23. Abdulateef Elbadawi and Hyder Mirghani. Assessment of HIV/AIDS comprehensive correct knowledge among Sudanese university: a cross-sectional analytic study 2014. Pan Afr Med J. 2016; 24: 48. doi: 10.11604/pamj.2016.24.48.8684

24. Mkumbo K. Assessment of HIV/AIDS knowledge, attitudes and behaviour among students in higher education in Tanzania. Glob Public Health. 2013;8(10):1168-79. doi: 10.1080/17441692.2013.837498.

25. Maimaiti N, Shamsuddin K, Abdurahim A, Tohti N, Maimaiti R. Knowledge, attitude and practice regarding HIV/AIDS among University students in Xinjiang. Global J Health Sci. 2010;2:51–60.

26. Unal Ayranci. AIDS knowledge and attitudes in a Turkish population: an epidemiological study. BMC Public Health20055:95. https://doi.org/10.1186/1471-2458-5-95.

27. Nubed CK, Akoachere JF. Knowledge, attitudes and practices regarding HIV/AIDS among senior secondary school students in Fako Division, South West Region, Cameroon. BMC Public Health. 2016 Aug 22;16(1):847. doi: 10.1186/s12889-016-3516-9. PubMed PMID: 27549185; PubMed Central PMCID:PMC4994230.

28. Shahla Soleymani et al. A cross-sectional study to explore postgraduate students' understanding of and beliefs about sexual and reproductive health in a public university, Malaysia. Reprod Health. 2015; 12: 77. Published online 2015 Aug 29. doi: 10.1186/s12978-015-0070-3

29. Badariah Mohd Saada, Peck-Leong Tan, Geetha Subramaniam. Implication of HIV/AIDS Knowledge on Quality of Life of Young Women in Malaysia. Procedia- Social and Behavioral Sciences 202 (2015) 218 – 226, https://doi.org/10.1016/j.sbspro.2015.08.225.

30. Karl Peltzer et al. Comparison of health risk behaviour, awareness, and health benefit beliefs of health science and non-health science students: An international study. Nursing

and Health Sciences (2016), 18, 180–187. DOI: 10.1111/nhs.12242.

APPENDICES

Questionnaire

Answer the following questions by ticking the box and please specify if you choose 'others'.

Demographic questions:

1) Age in years : _______

2) Gender   : [   ] Male   [   ] Female

3) Marital status : [   ] Single [   ] Married   [   ] Widowed   [   ] Divorced   [   ] Separated

4) Religion   : [   ] Muslim [   ] Christian [   ] Buddhist   [   ] Hindu

                [   ] Others: ______

5) Faculty   : [   ] Health Science   [   ] Non Health Science

6) Nationality   : [   ] Malaysian   [   ] Others: _________

7) Race   : [   ] Malay [   ] Chinese   [   ] Indian   [   ] Others:_________

General Knowledge about HIV/AIDS:

1	Do you know what the abbreviation of AIDS stands for?	YES	NO
2	Is AIDS a transmitted disease?	YES	NO
3	Is AIDS a hereditary disease?	YES	NO
4	Can HIV/ AIDS be cured at this moment?	YES	NO
5	Are there any vaccine for HIV/AIDS?	YES	NO

General public perception towards the possible causes of HIV infection:

1	Sexual intercourse without a condom with HIV infected person	YES		NO
2	Sharing needle with HIV infected person	YES		NO
3	Transfusion of HIV infected blood or receiving HIV infected organ	YES		NO
4	Having multiple sexual partners with unknown HIV status	YES		NO
5	From an HIV positive mother to her fetus	YES		NO
6	Sharing personal items such as shaving blades	YES		NO
7	Breast feeding from a HIV infected mother	YES		NO
8	Having tattoos or body piercings	YES		NO
9	Kissing an HIV infected person	YES		NO
10	Mosquito bites	YES		NO
11	Sharing/ eating a meal with an HIV infected person	YES		NO
12	Sharing water or drinks with an HIV infected person	YES		NO
13	Using public toilets	YES		NO
14	Casual contacts (hugging and touching) with an HIV infected person:	YES		NO

Respondents views about measures to prevent HIV infection:

1	Avoid taking illicit drugs/use of intravenous drugs	YES		NO
2	By avoiding sharing needles and syringes	YES		NO
3	Having sex with only one faithful, uninfected partner	YES		NO
4	Using condoms during sexual intercourse	YES		NO
5	Treating STDs promptly	YES		NO
6	Screening donated blood before transfusion	YES		NO
7	Not sharing toilets with an infected person	YES		NO
8	No sharing food with an infected person	YES		NO
9	Isolating people living with HIV/AIDS	YES		NO
10	Do not stay with infected person on same house	YES		NO
11	Do not have casual contact with infected person	YES		NO
12	Avoid mosquito bites	YES		NO

Misconceptions to person with HIV/ AIDS:

1	Love is a reason for HIV/ AIDS	YES		NO
2	AIDS is a punishment of God	YES		NO
3	AIDS can treated by holy water	YES		NO
4	AIDS do not come after marriage	YES		NO
5	AIDS can be transmitted by the cough	YES		NO

About the author

Associate Professor **Dr Mohammad Nazmul Hasan Maziz** is a Bangladeshi national and currently working as Deputy Dean and Head of Medical Microbiology Unit at Graduate School of Medicine, Perdana University, Malaysia. He is a very well-known academician and medical scientist.

www.ingramcontent.com/pod-product-compliance
Lightning Source LLC
Chambersburg PA
CBHW061324250726
48657CB00003B/1035